Are You the Missing Piece Workbook

By Viki Winterton

COPYRIGHT AND DISCLAIMER

ISBN-13: 978-1539078678

ISBN-10: 1539078671

Table of Contents

Introduction

Welcome to "Are You the Missing Piece Workbook." Turn your big idea into a book, a product, a business, a brand from Expert Insights!

You are in for an incredible experience unlike any you have previously encountered in any training program.

Everything you learn will enable you to stand out from the noise and have your potential clients almost naturally be drawn to you.

In each segment, you will experience a demonstration that will encompass almost every element of building your brand, business, project or book. From the beginning, you will envision your perfect business, how you develop a strong brand that influences your target market and then how to engage your following as clients for your books, products and services and maintain the relationship for the long term.

You will learn how to take the different tools and resources, time tested by the Fortune 500 and repurpose them for many situations you will experience with your clients in your business.

1. Authentic Attraction

Envisioning Your Purpose – Your Ideal Life / Story / Business

"This is the true joy in life, the being used for a purpose recognized by yourself as a mighty one."

—George Bernard Shaw

"I think the issue in our lives is greatness. When we connect to that, to our own unique knowledge that is within our life force, and we are aligned with it and we live in accordance with that inner blueprint, we create meaningful and satisfying lives, and we bring forth our greatness... Each of us is a unique combination... Not only is our DNA unique, but the entire expression of who we are is unique. We need all the pieces. When one person doesn't step out to be who they really are, you must realize that no one else can, and therefore there will be a hole there of something that did not contribute to the world. We will all suffer, and that's why I say "Who are you to deprive the world of your genius?"

—Dr. Joan King, Neuroscientist, MCC

"The most important project we could ever undertake is discovering who we really are, how we fit into the order of the universe, and what our particular purpose is in this life. We can ask our inner wisdom to reveal a vision of ourselves expressing our highest potential, our divine purpose".

"Our task, then, is to do whatever is necessary to help facilitate that purpose."

"Many of us get stuck in this step. Our highest vision for our lives may appear too big or overwhelming. Does achieving your highest potential bring up fear or discomfort? That's okay. That is proof you are moving toward and growing beyond the limited idea of who you thought you were."

—Coach Laurie Beth Jones

In Times of Uncertainty, the Best Career Defense is to Understand Your Life Purpose

The challenging assertions of a purposeful life include:

- *I work at what I love to do*
- *My daily choices are driven by a strong sense of purpose*
- *I am wholehearted and authentic in my actions and my words*
- *There is a clear alignment between what I say my priorities are and how I spend my time*
- *I invest time in making a difference to others in the world*
- *I put my whole self into all that I do*
- *I know what I want to be remembered for*

"...The most reliable insurance policy against being overwhelmed by sudden changes in one's environment is to return to life purpose. A sense of purpose is a personal compass to make your way through uncertain times."

—Career Expert and Coach Peter Sherer

Find / Rediscover the Passion in Your Work, the Purpose in Your Life, the Substance of Your Story

"Build your own dreams, or someone else will hire you to build theirs."
—Farrah Gray

Element	Action	Root Feelings
What You Love to Do A feeling of joy or fulfillment, the heart "sings" - something that creates a feeling of oneness with something or someone; time stops.		
What Is Unique About You? What are your unique gifts and talents? What's your contribution to make?		
Where Does Your Passion Reside What causes / issues are you most passionate about?		
What makes life worth living? Why do you get up every morning?		
What do you complain about the most? Is that something you would like to do something about?		
What 3 gifts of wisdom about life would you give to those who come to you?		
What are the 5 most important lessons you have learned in this life?		
Skills You Wish to Utilize These can be skills you currently possess or ones you wish to develop.		
Fields of Interest / Industries / Fields of Study What areas of interest do you currently have or wish to develop? What specific fields or industries might those relate to?		

Element	Action	Root Feelings
Education / Personal Growth What would be interesting to learn about? What would be ways to grow as a person?		
Work Values What is the most important thing to you in your work, your business?		
Personal Values What's most important in your life?		
Essence – Your Natural Qualities Example: Joy, caring, certainty, strength, discernment.		
Who You Would Like to Work With What kind of people do you want to work with?		
Compensation What do you need to receive to feel satisfied? Today? In the future?		
Working Conditions / Environment / Location Where and how would you like to work?		
Physical Health What level of health and vitality would you like to experience? What aspects of your health and body do you need to focus on?		
Mental / Emotional Health What mental or emotional states would you like to experience? What situations bring about these positive states of mind?		
Fun What brings a sense of fun, excitement, and new stimulation?		

Element	Action	Root Feelings
Ideal Lifestyle What is the most ideal lifestyle? What does life balance look like for you?		
Any Other Factors / Needs Example: A flexible schedule in order to be able to pick up children from day care or accommodate school life; need to be with like-minded people.		
Life Mission / Vision / Spiritual Path How would you like to contribute, what are you here to do?		
What do you want your life to stand for?		

Notes:

Discovering your life purpose comes down to 2 basic things:

  * Know yourself deeply
  * Know what you want

The more you know yourself, the more you are able to articulate what you want in life and from that will come discovering your purpose.

Listen. Listen to your own self. Quiet time allows you to hear your inner voice.

Stay Aware. Staying in present time allows you to notice in more detail what you are experiencing as you move through life, what you are experiencing from moment to moment.

Focus. If you can focus on your intention, listen, and remain aware, you may be surprised at how many choices open up as you move down the path of your purpose and passion.

My favorite exercises to keep your vision clear and on track:
Here are 7 Morning Power Questions Tony Robbins recommends:

  1. What am I happy about in my life now?
  2. What am I excited about in my life now?
  3. What am I proud about in my life now?
  4. What am I grateful about in my life now?
  5. What am I enjoying most in my life right now?
  6. What am I committed to in my life right now?
  7. Who do I love? Who loves me?

Here are 5 Problem Solving Questions to help you turn any situation around:

  1. What is great about this problem?
  2. What is not perfect yet?
  3. What am I willing to do to make it the way I want it?
  4. What am I willing to no longer do in order to make it the way I want it?
  5. How can I enjoy the process while I do what's necessary to make it the way I want it?

My Favorite Evening Questions:

What is the best thing that happened in my day? Why?
How did I create this?

Notes:

2. Your Brand

"Let the beauty we love be what we do." —Rumi

The Law of Compensation
Your business will be compensated to the degree that if satisfies three requirements:

1. There must be a strong desire in the market for your product or service.
2. Your service or product must be outstanding (excellence is a must).
3. You must be able to market and sell your offerings.

Marketing and sales are not about trying to convince or manipulate people into purchasing your service or product. They are about putting yourself out in front of and offering your services to those whom you are meant to do business with. To attract those who are already looking for your services.

Step 1. Identify your target market
The only way you will attract your ideal clients to your business is if you first create a crystal clear picture of who they are.

Exercise:
Who is your ideal client? Describe what he or she is like. Be creative and as detailed as possible.

Notes:

Step 2. Identify and understand your target market's most compelling needs and desires.

Hot buttons are the problems, frustrations, concerns and desires that matter most to your ideal client as they consider doing business with you. Their hot buttons are the driving force they have for doing business with you.

When you fully understand their hot buttons, your marketing message and activities will be targeted to your specific group of people. They will know you understand them and their concerns.

You must offer what your prospective clients want to buy, not what you want to sell or think they should buy.

Exercise:
What are your client's urgent needs?
What are your client's most compelling desires? What do they want to move toward?

Notes:

Step 3. Offer valuable services that solve their most pressing problem.

Do your services and products presently match the needs and wants of your target market with an ideal solution? What could you do that would create an extraordinary solution to that want and need?

Features are the tangible components of your product or service.
Advantages are the results produced by that product or service.
Benefits are the emotional experiences produced by those features and advantages.

Example:

Features: I meet with my clients three times per month, 250 pages of resource material, online application to stay on top of marketing activities.

Advantages: Clients put systems in place that makes their marketing effortless, they identify the marketing strategies that resonate with their personality.

Benefits: They become more confident about sales and marketing, they generate a more consistent pipeline of prospects, the average client increases their income by 50%.

Exercise:
List your services and products.

Features
What are the features of your product or service?
What is unique about you and your services?
Why should people work with you?

Advantages
What are the results they will get from working with you?

Notes:

Benefits

People buy things because of how those things make them feel. Think about the solutions you offer and the subsequent benefits they provide.

Clients want you to help them. Think of yourself as a trusted member of their professional team.

Benefits are normally related to an emotion. Example: My clients become more focused and take action that attracts business to them. The benefits are they experience a lot less stress, an increase in income and become much more confident.

What benefits do your clients experience from working with you?

Notes:

Step 4. Demonstrate the benefits your services provide.

Notes:

3. Your Niche

"When you follow your bliss... doors will open where you would not have thought there would be doors; and where there wouldn't be a door for anyone else."
—Joseph Campbell

When picking a specific Niche, be like the incredibly successful companies identified in Jim Collin's *Good to Great* and choose an area that:
_ You love and are passionate about.
_ You are great or can become great at.
_ People want, need, and are willing to pay for.

A big mistake often made when choosing a Niche is the belief that it must appeal to thousands and thousands of people. It doesn't!

For example, let's assume that your are targeting between 20-25 clients, and the average duration of the client relationship is six months. You only need to secure 40-50 new clients per year, or 3-4 clients per month. Forget about appealing to everyone! You want to pick a specific area and focus on finding 40-50 people who already want / need what you provide.

Choose one area of expertise! While this can be a challenge, your marketing efforts will be more effective if you provide a solution that helps your potential clients resolve one particular area of concern.

1. What do I love?
2. What am I great at?
3. What do people want and need that they are willing to pay for?

Notes:

_____
_____
_____
_____
_____

Exercise: Determine Your Niche
Use this chart as a tool to help you determine "what you do for your clients."

1. Fill out each column, focusing on one column at a time. For example, when you write down items under "What I Love," don't worry whether you are great at it or if people want, need and are willing to pay for it.

2. When you have listed things in all three columns, look to see if there are any congruencies.

What I Love	What I am Great At	What they want, need & willing to pay for

Possible Niches

Notes:

4. The Branding Process

"There is no passion to be found playing small – in settling for a life that is less than the one you are capable of living." —Nelson Mandela

Brand vs. Image

Your brand is what your clients think. Your image is what the client sees, hears or feels. Your Image makes your client envision your brand. This is why it is important to define your brand prior to designing your image. A mistake many make is to create an image with no foundation, making it all fluff.

Branding your name or your business name? Probably both!

Do you have a personal brand?
What do people think when they see or hear your name?
What do you want them to think?

Creating a personal brand can be of great benefit to your business. Your personal brand is your promise of service and value to your clients, vendors, readers and peers. A strong personal brand exposes your uniqueness and creates intrigue among your target market separating you from others with similar skills and abilities.

The brand building process:

Foundation Values: what matters most
Mission: the purpose for which you come to the party
Vision: where are you going

To define your personal brand, you have to look at who you are and what values, attributes, skills and strengths you bring to the table.

Your uniqueness comes from who you are and not what you do. For most of us, our uniqueness is second nature so it's not always easy to define that part of us that is powerful and memorable or in the minds of others.

But when you find a compelling way to articulate your talents and gifts, you will become fearless in articulating them.

Your personal brand strategy must be authentic.

1. Do your actions display your core values?
2. Are you synchronized or is something out of synch? This is important because if you are denying your core values and acting otherwise, those around you will sense something is off. And it may be difficult for them to do business with you.
3. Are you prepared for your best possible chance at success? Of all the things you may succeed at, those things that you are most passionate about give you the best possible chance.
4. What gets you up in the morning?
5. What topic could you discuss for hours?
6. In other words, what are you truly passionate about?
7. What is it you bring to the table for your clients?
8. What are your key talents and skills?
9. What is it that you are excellent at?

After you have asked yourself these questions, then ask family and friends to tell you what they think you are excellent at. Do your talents, skills, attributes and passions mesh well?

Notes:

Your personal brand should contain the intentions of your core values, passions and natural talents, and should express your key attributes. It will evolve over time and should support your mission and vision for yourself and your business. Think Oprah or Michael Jordan. Both have unique, memorable, established brands, supported by their appearance and actions.

The bottom line is simply to become the best "You." It is about finding your own personal essence that is at the same time valued by others.

> My brand is wrapped around my own personal values:
> empowerment, integrity, generosity and love.

Notes:

Step 1

Who are you?

If you were an existing brand product, what would that product be? Examples:
Are you Volvo... Safety or Nike ... Just Do It or Oprah...Inspirational?
Your brand message should create the same strong emotional bond.

Does that product speak to who you are?
What your personal values are?

Exercise:

Identify your core values: List the three or four that are central to who you are.
Examples: authenticity, generosity, honesty, integrity, success...

Do your actions display your core values? Are you synchronized or is something out of
synch? Once again, this is important because if you are denying your core values and
acting otherwise, those around you will sense something is off. And it may be difficult
for them to do business with you.

Notes:

Step 2

What gets you up in the morning? What topic could you discuss for hours?
In other words, what are you truly passionate about?

What do you bring to the table for your clients? What are your key talents and skills? What is it that you are really excellent at? Ask family and friends to tell you what they think you are excellent at. Examples: analytical, competence, team player, enthusiasm, risk taker...

Do your talents, skills, attributes and passions mesh well? Are there skills you may need to also be an expert in the area you are passionate about? If so, what could you do immediately to obtain that skill?

Do you see a specialty emerging here?

Notes:

Step 3
Write your brand description:
It should contain the intentions of your core values, passions and natural talents, and should express your key attributes.

Example: *"Great listener, role model, teacher and friend, Sally is authentic. She is generous and loving. She uses her coaching and writing to empower others and enjoys watching them blossom. Spirituality is important to her and her integrity is of the most importance in everything she does."*

Notes:

How do you create an image that will imprint the minds of your prospects?

According to Al Ries, author of *The 22 Immutable Laws of Branding*, branding in the marketplace is similar to branding on a ranch. A branding program must differentiate your cow from all the other cattle on the range, even if they all look pretty much the same. I don't necessarily like the analogy to cattle but it certainly gives us a clear picture.

Branding is a constant dripping of impressions on the prospect's mind. These impressions can be gathered from different places, your book, your newsletter, direct marketing piece, email signature, blog, auto responders or even a telephone contact. The consistency of these impressions is what helps people to feel familiar with your brand and the end result is a sense of comfort in buying from someone they are familiar with.

How do you begin the process of distinction that will allow people to associate with your unique identity? You begin with the basics: Your Company, your client and your competition. You must have a strong understanding of all three to develop a unique brand.

A great way to begin the process is to answer an important question: What problem does my customer / client have that I solve? You must be crystal clear with your answer and very succinct. Now how do you solve it? Again, it is very to the point as opposed to three paragraphs talking about all of your features.

Notes:

Now examine who you are:

· · What are your key business attributes?
· · How are you different from the competition?

Not only do you need to understand who you are, but also who your client is.

Notes:

Finally know your competition:
· ·How do they compare to you?
· ·How do clients perceive them?
· ·What do they do best?

If you have all of these answers, creating your unique identity will be easier. But make sure you are clear about this identity before you begin shouting it from the rooftops. Once clear, you can develop your brand strategy, your program of consistent touches.

Notes:

5. Your Mission Statement

*"The one thing that you have that nobody else has is you.
Your voice, your mind, your story, your vision.
So write and draw and build and play and dance and live as only you can."*
—Neil Gaiman

We started with your personal values, do they also hold true for your business? If so, it is time to define your mission.

Your mission statement defines the purpose of your business. It is written to serve you with an internal slogan of purpose, the center of focus and goal for your business. Start with your values and state who you are or who you want to be and then why your business was founded.

Remember having a mission statement and living it are two different things.

You may need two mission statements: a personal and a professional.
Personal: Have fun and inspire others to take action.

Professional: Become the number one choice for Solopreneur solutions for sales and marketing.

Notes:

Your Mission Statement: What your company does? Why? What makes it unique? Why should your audience care?	A company's mission statement is a constant reminder to its employees of why the company exists and what the founders envisioned when they put their fame and fortune at risk to breathe life into their dreams. **Samples:** *"To be the company of choice working in partnership with individuals and organizations to achieve their maximum potential."* *"Our mission is simple: to bring our customers powerful, on-demand conferencing technology backed by live, 24/7 support and unmatched attention to their needs."* **Your Mission Statement:**
Your Service / Product Intro:	Your company intro states in 30 seconds what you do, who benefits, how they benefit and an invitation for action. Clarity of your vision is required to create an effective company introduction. Sample: *"I have a calling. I am a customer satisfaction representative who calls customers to insure they're satisfied. "Yes" is my favorite word. What's yours?"* *"I turn conflict into agreement. My workshops and coaching reduce your conflict. We teach people how to understand, discuss and resolve conflict so they can live happier lives. Let us replace the conflict in your life."* **Your Intro**

Create your Mission statement: Why did I create this business / project?

Notes:

_____

_____

_____

_____

_____

_____

_____

_____

_____

_____

_____

_____

_____

_____

Create Your Intro

Notes:

_____

_____

_____

_____

_____

_____

_____

_____

_____

_____

_____

_____

6. Your Vision Statement

"I would rather die of passion than of boredom." —Vincent van Gogh

If Mission answers the question: What is my purpose or purpose of my business or project? Then Vision answers the question: How will I know when my mission has been accomplished?

Your vision statement is for you. The vision statement is a picture of your purpose fulfilled. It describes your desired future in clear terms, providing focus to your mission. Without it, you will not have a clear picture of where you are going. You will wind up somewhere—you just don't know where.

The key to creating a powerful brand is knowing what pond you want to be a big fish in, not attempting to be everything to everyone.

Notes:

Your Vision Summary: **Notes:**

Your personal goals:

Your financial goals:

Your spiritual goals:

Your strengths and abilities:

Your weakness:

Your specific target audience:

Your big idea:

Why Does Your Company / Project Exist?

What do you plan to do?

Who do you plan to do it for?

What best ensures success?

Exercise:
Create your Vision statement: Where do I want to be in the future?

Notes:

_____
_____
_____
_____
_____
_____
_____
_____
_____
_____
_____

Now your goals statement answers a different question: What steps must I take to get there? Take a quick snapshot of where you are now. Be honest with yourself and examine where you are within your market now. This will help you to identify your focus.

My Goals Statement as it relates to my branding strategy:

_____
_____
_____
_____
_____
_____
_____
_____
_____
_____

Are YOU the Missing Piece?
Don't Leave a Hole in the World

7. Your Marketing Plan

Idea Stage -	An idea has captured your attention and imagination
Planning Stage -	You determine the details associated with turning your idea into a viable business / project
Funding Stage -	Assessing and acquiring the money you need to start your business / project
Startup Stage -	Putting your plan into action
Ramp-up Stage -	Your business / project experiences rapid growth
Evolution Stage -	Balancing your current success with future growth

Notes:

_____
_____
_____
_____
_____
_____
_____
_____
_____
_____
_____
_____
_____

Your Marketing Plan Formula

There are a variety of styles and formats used for marketing plans. The following section headings will help you organize your plan. The content of the plan is much more important than rigid adherence to a specific format.

Executive Summary	The Executive Summary highlights the main goals and recommendations of the business or marketing plan. It should also briefly address budget requirements and how success will be measured.

Business Overview	This section is sometime referred to as the Situation Analysis segment. In a typical business or marketing plan, it contains relevant background on the market, product, pricing, and distribution situations as well as on competitors. Consider describing your customer base, services required by your customers, and your competition.

Competition Analysis	Review other major players in your marketplace – their strengths, weaknesses and overall success in the market. Their success can be an indication of yours.

Target Market	How well do you know your target market? How well do you understand their needs? Can you articulate what your customers and potential customers need as opposed to what you offer? Are there groups to whom you should be "selling" who are not now "buying" your services? Are there ways to segment your market so that you can offer highly specialized products and services to various groups, reflecting their business priorities? What kind of products should be offered to a broad base of users? Answering these questions will help you define your target market.

Goals	What do you want to achieve? The goal statement(s) should be challenging and yet, attainable.

Marketing Strategies	Strategies and programs which will help you reach the goals outlined above.

Implementation Tactics	Tasks required to implement and monitor each strategy are listed in this section. With each task, the person responsible for the task, and a completion target date are indicated. Having a plan of action with specific tasks ensures that the details are clear and that specific persons are accountable for easy management and completion.

Strategy 1	Description	Start Date	Responsible	Target Date	Completed
Task 1	Revise Profile	12/1/10	Viki	12/15/10	12/14/10
Task 2					
Task 3					
Task 4					
Task 5					
Task 6					

Strategy 2	Description	Start Date	Responsible	Target Date	Completed
Task 1					
Task 2					
Task 3					
Task 4					
Task 5					
Task 6					

Operations Plan	Provide your service providers and operational procedures. Will you operate from a home office or require office space? Are you a one-person-show or will you need support? Employees or VA / Temp Help? What other office, product and operational expenses will you incur?

Operations	Description	Vendor	Reoccurring	Amount	Frequency
Expense 1					
Expense 2					
Expense 3					
Expense 4					
Expense 5					
Expense 6					

Budget	How much will the operational and marketing activities defined above cost? Can you provide a revenue forecast? Explain the assumptions on which the forecast is based and consider various (best case, worst case) scenarios.

Evaluation of Results	What are the success criteria? How will you measure success of the plan? By monitoring progress, you can judge the success of the plan. If some of the strategies are not working out, try to determine why. Is the strategy flawed? Is there a problem with implementation or timing? How can you refocus and move on?

Risks & Opportunities	What is your SWOT Analysis, (Strengths, Weaknesses, Opportunities, and Threats.) Reflect on current strengths, weaknesses and special opportunities of your venture, as well as opportunities and threats to be dealt with in the coming year.

The Management Team	Why are you, your partners and your advisory team the most qualified group to start and run this business? Getting clear on this area will give you a great marketing platform and also tell you what you may need in the way of information, education and support to achieve your goals.

Notes:

8. Building Your Brand Visually

Remember: Your image is what the client sees, hears or feels. When what the client sees, hears and feels all match up with your brand, this builds a sense of trust and loyalty. People feel comfortable and confident that you are who you say you are and that you can deliver what they need. Imagine how it is to do business with someone you trust! That person is easy to say "yes" to.

Logo, web and print design which attracts and engages your ideal clients and radiates the spirit of your work is a key factor in building a strong brand. This influences both how much success you will enjoy and how much ease and flow you will experience in your business.

This is good news! Choosing how you and your business are represented visually empowers you to attract positive experiences.

Building a strong brand will skyrocket your business. Get ready to explore!

My Brand:
In step 3, you determined your brand description.

> My brand description ...

Support Materials:
Your logo, web site and marketing materials speak volumes about you to your prospects ... often before you even get to say a word! They will support and enhance your brand.

Poorly-designed support materials make prospects take you less seriously, erode trust or lead them to believe that you may do an inferior job for them. Well-designed support materials will convey to people your unique gifts and the benefits of doing business with you.

Make sure you're sending the right message!

Which of the following support materials do you already have?
If you have these materials but they don't reflect your brand description, check the "need" column.

Have	Need	Support Materials	Does it accurately reflect my brand description?
		Logo	
		Web site	
		Blog	
		Ezine / newsletter	
		Online advertising	
		Video promotions	
		e-Book	
		Business card	
		Letterhead	
		Envelopes	
		Flyers / promotional material	
		Print advertising	
		Book	
		CD / audio product	
		Other:	

Hiring a Designer

When you choose a graphic designer to help you create the imagery which accompanies your marketing materials, make sure that you feel comfortable with them ... you feel heard, they "get" you and they have the experience to do a professional job for you. You're building a relationship. And if they "get" you, they can help your ideal clients to "get" you.

Don't worry if you feel unclear on what steps you need to take or how best to represent your brand through images. Your designer is your teammate. An experienced designer has been through this process many times and can guide you, tell you what to expect and hold your hand should you need it.

4 things to look for when hiring a designer

1. Experience: You want to work with someone who understands the snafus that can arise and who knows how to make your project run as smoothly as possible. Working with someone who has experience offers superior results for you and your business. Plus, it makes the design process a positive and enjoyable experience for you.
Ask:
How long have you been in business? Is this a full time or a part time gig for you? If part time, why is that?

2. Original design: It's important that your brand is clearly YOUR brand. Would it concern you if you paid someone to design a logo or web banner for you and then next month you see the same artwork on someone else's site?
If so, ask:
Do you draw or illustrate? Do you use clip art, stock photography or templates? Do I have exclusive rights to the artwork that you create for me?

3. Communication: Do you feel comfortable when you talk with the designer? Make sure you feel that they're listening to what you say. It's important that the communication flows. If they're going to help you successfully express who you are to your clients, they need to understand who you are and to ask the right questions to find out. A good designer will find out what's important to you, contribute their own creative spin, and then incorporate your feedback.
Ask:
What is your process? How do you work? What happens if I want you to change something?

4. Creativity: Do you like their work? Each project is unique so even if they haven't done the exact thing you're looking for visually, if you like their other work and appreciate their design sense, most likely they could deliver something you'll really love. When working on your project, a good designer will show you a range of options to choose from.

Ask:

May I see your portfolio?

When working on a project, do you show the client a number of design directions?

Notes:

The Creative Brief:

When you get really clear about your visual image, your designer can create a logo, web site or marketing materials which bring your dream to life, express the essence of your spirit and attract clients who are just perfect for you. Bring this worksheet to your designer to help him / her connect with your vision.

This can be a fun adventure so just close your eyes for a moment ... Imagine how you are going to feel whenever you reach out to your ideal client with visuals which radiate your very own energy right there with you, backing you up. Feels good, right? Let's get started!

You and Your Big Dreams:
• What would you love for your visuals to say about you?
• How would you describe yourself to your clients or clients?
• Who would you like to appeal to? Describe your ideal client in detail.
• What is your mission?
• What would you like people to feel when they experience your work?
• What are your objectives? What is your big dream?
• Which three words or phrases best describe the spirit of you and your work?
• How would you like to be perceived?
• Who do you admire in your area of expertise? Who is doing what you do?
  What is it that you like most about what they're doing?
• What is special and unique about you? What sets you apart from others?

Vision:
• Describe what you envision for your logo / web site.
• What concept would you like the imagery to express?
• Are there any specific icons / symbols which you'd like to be incorporated? Why?
• Are there any specific icons / symbols which you'd absolutely not want used? Why?

Color:
• What color(s) do you feel best represent the spirit of your work and why? (Answer intuitively.)
• Are there any colors you would absolutely not want to be used and why?
• After reviewing this, which colors now resonate?

Visual Style:

- What type of artwork or imagery really sings to your soul? (example: whimsical, geometric)
- What is it that you love about that style? Which book covers, logos or web sites do you like?
- Do you have any general likes or dislikes concerning colors, images, typography, etc.?

Notes:

The Eight Laws of Personal Branding
by Peter Montoya

1. The Law of Specialization: A great Personal Brand must be precise, concentrated on a single core strength, talent or achievement. You can specialize in one of many ways: ability, behavior, lifestyle, mission, product, profession or service.

2. The Law of Leadership: Endowing a Personal Brand with authority and credibility demands that the source be perceived as a leader by the people in his / her domain or sphere of influence. Leadership stems from excellence, position or recognition.

3. The Law of Personality: A great Personal Brand must be built on a foundation of the source's true personality, flaws and all. It is a law that removes some of the pressure laid on by the Law of Leadership: you've got to be good, but you don't have to be perfect.

4. The Law of Distinctiveness: An effective Personal Brand needs to be expressed in a way that is different from the competition. Many marketers construct middle-of-the-road brands so as not to offend anyone. This is a route to failure because their brands will remain anonymous among the multitudes.

5. The Law of Visibility: To be successful, a Personal Brand must be seen over and over again, until it imprints itself on the consciousness of its domain or sphere of influence. Visibility creates the presumption of quality. People assume because they see a person all the time, he / she must be superior to others offering the same product or service.

6. The Law of Unity: The private person behind a Personal Brand must adhere to the moral and behavioral code set down by that brand. Private conduct must mirror the public brand.

7. The Law of Persistence: Any Personal Brand takes time to grow, and while you can accelerate the process, you can't replace it with advertising or public relations. Stick with your Personal Brand, without changing it; be unwavering and be patient.

8. The Law of Goodwill: A Personal Brand will produce better results and endure longer if the person behind it is perceived in a positive way. He / she must be associated with a value or idea that is recognized universally as positive and worthwhile.

"Regardless of age, regardless of position, regardless of the business we happen to be in, all of us need to understand the importance of branding. We are CEOs of our own companies: Me Inc. To be in business today, our most important job is to be head marketer for the brand called You." —Tom Peters in Fast Company

Notes:

9. Authentic Network Communication

"Regardless of the changes in technology,
the market for well-crafted messages will always have an audience."
— Steve Burnett, The Burnett Group

Communication and the Web –

Social networks on the web have become thoroughly embedded in contemporary culture. Your future clients have woven these networks into their daily routines, using Facebook, Twitter, YouTube, LinkedIn and other tools to build and maintain complex webs of professional and personal relationships. Not incorporating these tools in your marketing plan is a **huge missed opportunity** to communicate with your target audience.

How can Social Media Help
- Research and learn
- Study your competition
- Develop your plan
- Position yourself and your business
- Communicate and participate
- Build visibility and credibility
- Influence and sell
- Grow and prosper

How can Social Media Impact your Marketing Plan in a new way today:

Notes:

Your Target Market - Where Are They?

Keep it simple

- **Blogs**
Blogging has developed into a popular way for people to publish content online. A blog is simply a set of Web pages that are often written in a diary-like form. People writing blogs typically comment on current events, their lives, new ideas and gadgets, trends, ongoing news stories, and any number of topics. (WordPress, Blogger, etc.)

- **Online Social Networks**
Creating social groups is one of the original practices on the Internet. People have consistently used online tools to expand, extend, re-invent, and build social groups. Today, social networking has become a major activity online, and a strong business awareness builder. (LinkedIn, Facebook, niche sites)

- **Micro Blogs**
Microblogging is a form of blogging. A microblog differs from a traditional blog in that its content is typically much smaller, in both actual size and aggregate file size. A microblog entry could consist of nothing but a short sentence fragment, or an image or embedded video. (Twitter)

- **Video**
Web video offers an important opportunity for small businesses to connect with a wider audience. For small business owners, online video represents a chance to reach thousands or potentially millions of people using a relatively simple and inexpensive format. (YouTube)

Your Target Audience - Find Them

The Internet is an utterly fantastic resource for topic research. Browse around for your target market's discussion groups, and see what people are talking about. Look for groups that have a lot of members, and keep track of the subjects discussed.

There are three basic types of search tools that most people use to find what they are looking for on the Web (there's more than this, but these are the basics that everyone should start with):

- Search Engines
  Search engines are large, <u>spider</u> created databases of web pages that help searchers find specific information on any given subject. You type in a keyword or phrase and the search engine retrieves pages that correspond to your search query. <u>www.google.com</u>

- Subject Directories
  <u>Subject directories</u> in general are smaller and more selective than search engines. They use categories to focus your search, and their sites are arranged by categories, not just by keywords. Subject directories are handy for broad searches, as well as finding specific web sites. Most subject directories' main purpose is to be informational, rather than commercial. A good example of a search directory is <u>www.yahoo.com</u>, a combination search engine / search directory / search portal.

- MetaSearch Tools
  Metasearch engines get their search results from several search engines. Users will receive the best hits to their keywords from each search engine. Metasearch tools are a good place to start for very broad results, but do not (usually) give the same quality results as using each search engine and directory. <u>www.dogpile.com</u>

About your market – Keyword Searches

What do they want? What do they need? What are they talking about? What do they find exciting, interesting? What are their dreams? What keeps them up at night? What is their language? What are their needs that aren't being met? What is the hot topic NOW?

There are two reasons to start with audience needs, rather than jumping straight into keyword research:

1. Content Strategy: You want to provide content and tools that are as relevant and useful as possible to your target audience.
2. Targeted Keyword Discovery: Ideally, you'll want to do keyword research based on what the audience wants, not solely on what content your marketing already has or you plan to have, which may be limited.

A great keyword niche finding tool:
http://www.wordstream.com/keyword-niche-finder/?src=adwords&cmp=keyword-tool&gclid=CLzH2PW00qMCFcrD7QoduUlLtg

What key words around your target market's pain points will you use for your search? Will you use to help your target market find you?

Notes:

Clarify your message

Social media is a valuable medium for carrying key messages, building relationships and increasing service / product loyalty. But that's what it is – a medium. What doesn't change is the core work of examining the marketing strategy, crafting transparent and clear messages, and then engaging social media to add value and build relationships.

What are you selling?

Who are you selling to?

What are they really buying emotionally?

What benefits are you providing?

How?

Notes:

Increase your visibility and influence - Make it easy for people to find you

Network profiles

A profile creates opportunities for the exchange of ideas and knowledge on social networks. It is not a resume – it acts as your marketing collateral. A well-constructed profile creates the impression of value to a networking relationship.

Networking groups

Effective networking is the foundation of successful small business marketing for service professionals.

Get connected with prospects and people who know members of your target market to build your list of contacts and to increase your opportunities and increase profits. Grow and build these valuable contacts through frequent and personalized communication.

Your own network

If you would like to develop you own network, we found that www.Ning.com provides the best platform for setting up good-looking, sophisticated social networks with minimal effort. For network and site hosting, http://www.earthgrid.com is superb.

Many niche networks, LinkedIn and Facebook also provide "groups" where you can kickoff your network as part of a larger venue.

Keyword searches - Use this great search tool to look for networks: (http://freekeywords.wordtracker.com)

Show your social media presence on your blog, on your website and on your emails. Drive links to your social media activities from site icons. http://webdesignledger.com/freebies/the-best-social-media-icons-all-in-one-place

Social Media DOs

- Share the full dimension of YOU

- Be authentic – be human

- Provide quality content

- Add links so people can find you easily

- Post comments / opinions relevantly associated with hot topics.

- Foster curiosity with small pieces of valuable info

- Maintain open and frequent communication

- Give your fans and followers some exposure

Social Media DON'Ts

- Politics, Religion and Sex – unless that's your biz

- Excessive games, jokes, and viral marketing

- Links, links and only links

- Publicly thanking others for praise of you

- Canned Direct Messages

- Business only promotion

- Inconsistent, unclear message / brand

- Connecting with those with 'numbers' only

- Follow everyone's advice – learn the basics – develop your own platform

Using Your Resources to the Max

Get and post specific testimonials from happy customers – whenever possible:
Include $s saved
Cite numbers increased

Foster referrals
Ask for them
Develop an affiliate program

Enter joint ventures and strategic alliances
Who does business with your target audience?
Who makes money when you do?
Trade services and research free expert advice!

My plan for fostering testimonials, referrals and JVs:

Notes:

Favorite Social Media Tools

See who tweeting about you
http://search.twitter.com/

Find out whose searching for you
http://www.google.com/alerts

Post your messages in advance and vet followers
www.socialoomph.com

Monitor and control postings from desktop
http://seesmic.com/

*"The basic building block of good communications is the feeling
that every human being is unique and of value."*
— Unknown

*"You can have brilliant ideas, but if you can't get them across,
your ideas won't get you anywhere."*
— Lee Iacocca

10. Active Marketing Strategy – Strategic Alliances

An **alliance** is an agreement between two or more parties, made in order to advance common goals and to secure common interests.

A **strategy** is a plan of action designed to achieve a particular goal.

A **Strategic Alliance** is a formal relationship between two or more parties to pursue a set of agreed upon goals or to meet a critical business need while remaining independent organizations.

A typical strategic alliance formation process involves these steps:

- **Strategy Development**: Strategy development involves studying the alliance's feasibility, objectives and rationale, focusing on the major issues and challenges and development of resource strategies for production, technology, and people. It requires aligning alliance objectives with the overall corporate strategy.

- **Partner Assessment**: Partner assessment involves analyzing a potential partner's strengths and weaknesses, creating strategies for accommodating all partners' management styles, preparing appropriate partner selection criteria, understanding a partner's motives for joining the alliance and addressing resource capability gaps that may exist for a partner.

- **Contract Negotiation**: Contract negotiations involves determining whether all parties have realistic objectives, forming high calibre negotiating teams, defining each partner's contributions and rewards as well as protect any proprietary information, addressing termination clauses, penalties for poor performance, and highlighting the degree to which arbitration procedures are clearly stated and understood.

- **Alliance Operation**: Alliance operations involves addressing senior management's commitment, finding the calibre of resources devoted to the alliance, linking of budgets and resources with strategic priorities, measuring and

rewarding alliance performance, and assessing the performance and results of the alliance.

- **Alliance Termination**: Alliance termination involves winding down the alliance, for instance when its objectives have been met or cannot be met, or when a partner adjusts priorities or re-allocates resources elsewhere.

The advantages of strategic alliance includes 1) allowing each partner to concentrate on activities that best match their capabilities, 2) learning from partners and developing competences that may be more widely exploited elsewhere, 3) suitability of the resources and competencies of an organization for it to survive.

There are four types of strategic alliances: joint venture, equity strategic alliance, non-equity strategic alliance, and global strategic alliances.

Joint venture is a strategic alliance in which two or more firms create a legally independent partnership to share some of their resources and capabilities to develop a competitive advantage. ~ *Wikipedia's explanation*.

Notes:

Professionally Structured

It is especially important for a Strategic Alliance to be effective that it is professionally structured.

Partnering Code of Conduct
1. Be the kind of partner with whom you'd like to partner.
2. Ethics and morals are important.
3. Respect others — their beliefs, customs and policies.
4. Think as a member of both your alliance and your industry.
5. When in doubt, don't!

Notes:

Systematic

In order for a Strategic Alliance to be most effective, you need a system by which the STRATEGIC ALLIANCE PARTNER refers people to you. The referring process must become a part of their business. It should not be an afterthought, or when it comes to mind, or when they think there may be a perfect fit. Instead, imagine every single one of their clients being systematically, professionally and attractively introduced to you and your services.

Example

Jane sends a letter to 21 CPAs in the area, inviting them to lunch to explore the possibility of forming a strategic partnership. She selected CPAs because she specializes in coaching entrepreneurial start-ups on sales and marketing. Jane realized that CPAs are one of the first stops many new businesses make, thus they deal directly with her target market.

She receives 7 responses. After having the lunch meetings, there seems to be a great fit with one of the CPAs. Jane drafts an agreement, spelling out their commitments to one another. Jane is providing free coaching to the owner and staff. They meet two times per month to strategize, implement and fine-tune their "Exposure Strategies," which include a direct mail postcard to all of the CPA's clients, a monthly lecture series on sales and marketing, staff training on offering Comp Sessions and properly placed brochures. The STRATEGIC ALLIANCE PARTNER receives a 10% referral fee from all sales that are generated from their relationship.

Characteristics

- The STRATEGIC ALLIANCE PARTNER's clients are congruent with Jane's Who and What.
- The relationship is structured and professional.
- There is a solid, structured marketing plan in place.
- The staff is trained.
- The Strategic Partner benefits.

Benefits of Forming Powerful Strategic Alliances

As you can imagine, there are many benefits of forming powerful Strategic Alliances. Here are our "Top 3." We encourage you to come up with more, so <u>you feel</u> how powerful these can be!

"Triple Win"

Marketing strategies are most effective when everybody wins. In fact, we often refer to Strategic Alliances as a "Triple Win." For now, we want you to think about how very important it is for the Strategic Alliance to be taken seriously and the referral process to become part of the STRATEGIC ALLIANCE PARTNER's business. This only happens if he is receiving a benefit or some other "reward" for his efforts!

Exposure / Multiple Complimentary Sessions

The Complimentary Session is the cornerstone of the system. When you perform numerous Comp Sessions, you get multiple clients. It is that simple. What you are looking for in a Strategic Alliance is the opportunity to be introduced to their clients. Your goal is exposure. The beauty and magic of the Complimentary Session to take care of the rest!

An effective Strategic Alliance allows you to be exposed to dozens, even hundreds, of people. You then perform Comp Sessions and secure multiple clients from the one relationship. This is so much easier and more effective than looking to secure one client at a time!

Credibility Factor

Strategic Alliances are particularly effective because the STRATEGIC ALLIANCE PARTNER has credibility with her clients, so when she refers them to you, they are receptive. If it is a trusting relationship, the clients will often follow the recommendation of the STRATEGIC ALLIANCE PARTNER!

Make relationship bank deposits before you try to make a withdrawal.

How To Develop Strategic Alliances

Step 1 - Identify Potential Strategic Alliances

Look for companies that have a similar customer base to yours and enter into a discussion about how to work together.

Before entering into a strategic alliance, enough thought is to be placed behind the structure of the relationship and the details of how it will be managed. Consider the following in your planning process:

- define expected outcomes from the relationship for all the parties in the strategic alliance
- define and document the elements provided by each party, and the benefits a successful alliance brings to each
- identify the results that will cause the alliance to be most beneficial for your business and define the structure and operating issues that need to be addressed to achieve these results

You need to have a specific target market and niche in order to identify the best possible Strategic Alliance Partners. Your goal is to identify the types of businesses who serve the same target market as you do! Right now we are not looking for specific people who you may know. Instead, identify ideas and opportunities.

For example, let's say you coach small business owners. What type of professionals already have a favorable relationship with small business owners? How about accountants? Especially those who specialize in small business owners! Financial Planners also come to mind, as well as printers, bankers, web designers, the Chamber of Commerce and attorneys.

Imagine, for example, forming a strong Strategic Alliance with a successful and trusted accountant who has 200 small business owners as clients. The accountant fully believes and supports your coaching and systematically informs all of his clients about your services and funnels them into Complimentary Sessions.

Or, let's say you are a graphics designer who works with small service-based companies. Imagine forming an alliance with a copywriting service, a printer or the Chamber of Commerce. The opportunities are endless!

Step 2 - Craft and Send Inquiry Letter

Once you have identified opportunities that are congruent with your target market and niche, it is time to craft a letter and reach out to your potential STRATEGIC ALLIANCE PARTNERs. Please note, even though the Strategic Alliance relationship is win-win-win, not everybody is going to be receptive to your inquiry. This is important so that you do not "put all of your eggs in one basket." Like the sales process, it is a numbers game, so the more people you reach out to, the more likely you are to ultimately have success.

We are assuming that you do not have a personal relationship with your prospective STRATEGIC ALLIANCE PARTNERs. If you do, of course reach out to them first! An existing relationship or a referral will dramatically improve the likelihood of securing a meeting to explore the opportunity.

Keys for a Successful Inquiry Letter

1. **Be brief**. The goal is to set up a meeting to discuss the alliance. You are not looking to sell them in this initial contact, instead just spark their interest.

2. **Explicitly state** that you are *not* trying to sell them anything.

3. Present a few of your ideas on **how the relationship can benefit them**. People are most interested in the "WIIFM" ("what's in it for me?") principle. Tell them!

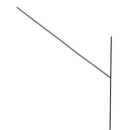

Be clear about what you want from your alliance relationship and what you are willing to give to it.

Sample Inquiry Letter

Dear Mr. Smith,

I have a rather unusual proposition for you. It's something that I believe could provide a great deal of profit to you with absolutely no risk.

My name is {your name} and I'm the owner of {your company name}.

We're {mention one or two things about your company and what you do}. And as you can see, our {products/services} seem very complementary to what you offer. That's why I wanted to write and introduce you to an idea that could create another source of revenue for you while providing a valuable service to your customers.

Mr. Smith, I am not looking to sell you anything. Rather, I believe my {product or service} would be of tremendous benefit to your customers/clients and I am willing to compensate you greatly for referrals. The best thing would be for us to meet for 30 minutes and I will share with you some of my ideas, but here are just some of the ways you could benefit:

- Passive income by receiving a referral fee from me.
- Complimentary {product or service}.
- Cross promotion to my client database of {description}.
- Complimentary or reduced fee consulting services.
- Any combination of the above.

These are just examples, as we would co-create a plan that is best for you. I am very adaptable. We will also discuss creating a system whereby my introduction to your clients is done in an attractive, non-threatening way. All I am looking for is exposure. I will take it from there.

If this sounds like a good idea (and it really is), I'd like to discuss it with you personally. I'll give you a call next Monday at 9:00am to schedule a time we can meet. Please ask your secretary to be expecting my call. Or if you prefer, you can call me at {xxx-xxx-xxxx}. I look forward to meeting with you.

Sincerely,

<Your name>

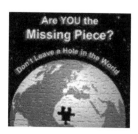

Step 3 - Make Follow Up Phone Calls

You must follow up your Inquiry Letter with a phone call! In fact, if you are not willing to make follow-up phone calls, we'll even go as far as to say don't even bother writing and sending an Inquiry Letter! We know this may sound extreme; however, people are busy and in this case, we are assuming that the potential Strategic Alliance Partner does not know you. In this scenario, a letter on its own will rarely generate a response. Therefore you must follow up!

The best way to follow up is with a phone call. It is important to mix your "touches," as people respond differently to different forms of communication. In addition, you cannot form an effective Strategic Alliance without having a conversation, so once your initial inquiry is made via letter it is time to get on the phone!

Keys for Successful Follow Up

Here is how we recommend following up and what we have found works best. This approach has been tested in several industries and is excellent for people who aren't necessarily excited about sales and marketing.

Block Out Time for Follow Up

You must block out time on a weekly basis for following up on your marketing strategies, whatever they may be. Our studies show that, on average, you can make 10-15 follow-up phone calls per hour, so budget your time accordingly. If you sent out 30 letters, budget 3-4 hours of time. (This assumes that more than half of the people will not be available and you will leave messages 60% of time.)

Reward Yourself

This is the toughest part for most people. I encourage you to read your belief narrative, repeat your affirmations and do some deep breathing or meditating to help you relax. You may also want to incorporate a reward for after you have completed your follow-up calls. What do you really enjoy doing that you don't treat yourself enough with? Bubble bath, massage, walk in the park, new book, etc. The key is to reward yourself! Make your business building fun!

Prepare / Fine Tune Your Script

Use the example below and create a script based on your unique personality and style. As you gain more experience, you will quickly learn what you are most comfortable with and what works best. Relax, be yourself and have fun! People will be most attracted to you when you use a natural, comfortable approach that fits who you really are.

Visualize

As is true with every form of follow up, it is very important that you vividly visualize a smooth flowing conversation. We recommend doing a "master visualization" prior to all of your calls and a "mini" visualization prior to each call.

Please do not skip this step! As a coach, we trust that you know the importance of leveraging the power of your mind. You get what you think about. The energy that is sent to the Universe connects with your contact and produces a powerful result.

Make The Call!

Well, the only thing left is to "smile and dial!"

Notes:

Sample Follow-Up Phone Scripts

Following are some sample scripts for your follow-up calls. There are a vast array of potential paths your calls can take, and we do not want to write a book on word-for-word scripts covering every scenario. Rather use these as a guide to get the ball rolling. With practice, you will quickly get into a flow that is congruent with your particular style.

If you leave a recorded message, we recommend you say something similar to this:

> "Hello Mr. Johnson. This is Viki Winterton with EIP. I am the publisher who sent you a letter last week about forming a Strategic Alliance together. Just following up to see if you were intrigued. Mr. Johnson, I am very confident that a Strategic Alliance can benefit you in a variety of ways, as well as your clients. I'd love to have a call to discuss this further. Would you please call me back at xxx-xxx-xxxx. Again my name is Viki Winterton and I can be reached at xxx-xxx-xxxx. Thanks and have a great day."

When you do get through, we recommend a very similar approach:

> "Hello, Mr. Johnson. This is Viki Winterton with EIP. I am the publisher who sent you the letter last week about forming a mutually beneficial Strategic Alliance. Were you intrigued by the letter?

> I am a (   ) who specializes in (   ). I think I can be of tremendous service to your clients and I am willing to reward you in a number of ways for referrals. Does this interest you?"

> May I take you to lunch so we can get to know one another and discuss this in more detail?

The key is to find out gauge their interest. Next you want to summarize the key points of the letter and set up a time to meet with them!

Step 4 - Meet with the Prospective Strategic Alliance Partner

What an exciting opportunity, to meet with a prospective Strategic Alliance Partner! Remember, this one relationship can potentially fill your practice! Not to say that in order for a Strategic Alliance to be effective, you need to experience this level of success. Any exposure to prospective clients is a win for you. Remember, all you are looking for is exposure, the opportunity to have a conversation with a prospect. You will take it from there!

Do not feel like you need to have everything figured out before you set up your meetings. This may paralyze you and keep you from reaching out. This is an exploratory meeting. You are looking to get to know one another, for you to share the beauty of coaching, to learn about their business and if there is a fit, to co-create your professional relationship.

The term "co-create" is key! Use what you learn in this class to prepare for the initial meeting. Give thought to ways the partnership can be structured and how you would like to "reward" the STRATEGIC ALLIANCE PARTNER. Then, at the meeting, <u>be a coach</u> and discover what the STRATEGIC ALLIANCE PARTNER really wants and how he / she would most like to benefit from the Strategic Alliance. From there, the two of you can co-create a customized Strategic Alliance that is truly win-win-win.

Ways the STRATEGIC ALLIANCE PARTNER Can "Win"

We have identified several ways a Strategic Alliance Partner can benefit from forming a relationship with you. We strongly encourage you to use these ideas to spur your thinking so you can truly customize your partnership to best create the Triple Win and serve the needs of the STRATEGIC ALLIANCE PARTNER. The more the STRATEGIC ALLIANCE PARTNER "wins," the more he / she will do his / her part to make the partnership work and refer people to you.

Goodwill

For example, if you focused on coaching divorced women to help them rebuild their life after divorce, you could structure a Strategic Alliance with a divorce attorney. Do you think that the attorney benefits from being a caring, compassionate, supportive attorney who partners his clients with a coach? Then, not only would the attorney handle the legal side of the divorce, but he could also market himself as an attorney who really cares!

Refer Clients to Strategic Alliance Partner

A quick and easy benefit to the STRATEGIC ALLIANCE PARTNER is a reciprocal referral arrangement, whereby you refer your clients to them.

Coaching Services

Another way the STRATEGIC ALLIANCE PARTNER can "win" is by receiving free or discounted coaching, either for himself and / or his staff. Let's say you charge $350 per month for coaching and you coach the STRATEGIC ALLIANCE PARTNER for 6 months.

The STRATEGIC ALLIANCE PARTNER would receive $2,100 worth of services! That is a lot of money! If the system is set up in the right way, it is a nice exchange for very little work. This, of course, does not even take into account the improvements in the business the STRATEGIC ALLIANCE PARTNER can make due to your coaching. Perhaps his business will improve by $20,000 during that 6-month period. Not bad for referring you some clients!

Consulting / Work Project

Yet another way to provide value to the STRATEGIC ALLIANCE PARTNER is by consulting or doing some type of work for them. What expertise could you offer a STRATEGIC ALLIANCE PARTNER? Perhaps you could help them design their website, do research, help them with marketing, organize their office. The possibilities are endless!

Pay a Referral Fee

Let's begin with a question: Would you rather earn $300 per month per client and have to do all of the marketing yourself, or would you rather earn $250 per month, pay a $50 referral fee per month and have a steady stream of potential clients referred to you?

There are a number of ways to determine the referral fee and the key is, of course, to co-create it with the STRATEGIC ALLIANCE PARTNER. In general, we recommend 20%-30% of your fees be given to the STRATEGIC ALLIANCE PARTNER in exchange for the referral.

At first glance, it may seem quite generous to give the STRATEGIC ALLIANCE PARTNER 30%. We agree, it is generous! And, you need to impact the STRATEGIC ALLIANCE PARTNER so you stay in the forefront of their mind and send people your way!

Note: Some professionals are prohibited by law from receiving referral fees. Research this before you send your inquiry letter. For example, you do not want to suggest giving a referral fee to a psychotherapist – one profession we know of that is prohibited from receiving referral fees.

Note: When offering a referral fee, do NOT inflate your fees in a Strategic Alliance arrangement in order to make your same rate. For example, if you normally charge $300/month, do not charge clients referred by your STRATEGIC ALLIANCE PARTNER $370 per month, so that you can pay the STRATEGIC ALLIANCE PARTNER $70 and still make your target of $300.

Critical Success Factors For Successful Strategic Alliances

The STRATEGIC ALLIANCE PARTNER Must Understand the Benefits and Value of Your Offering

To maximize the success of a Strategic Alliance, you want your STRATEGIC ALLIANCE PARTNER to become a "Raving Fan." It is one thing for a STRATEGIC ALLIANCE PARTNER to refer people to you from time-to-time because they are your friend, or because you asked them to, or because they get a referral fee. It is quite another thing when the STRATEGIC ALLIANCE PARTNER is getting coached by you and is receiving tremendous benefit themselves! It is important that they be able to communicate to their clients the benefits of coaching. The more understanding, energy and excitement your STRATEGIC ALLIANCE PARTNER has about your coaching, the better!

Personal Recommendation

The KEY to really making this work is for the STRATEGIC ALLIANCE PARTNER to personally recommend you to all of his / her clients.

Referral System

Ideally, you want to develop a structured and systematic process by which the STRATEGIC ALLIANCE PARTNER sends you referrals. You do not want the referral process to be left to chance. For example, only when the STRATEGIC ALLIANCE PARTNER thinks of it. Here are some examples of what we mean by systematized:

Visible Brochure

Your brochure and / or promotional materials should be made available to the STRATEGIC ALLIANCE PARTNER's clients. Create an attractive display case and have them in the lobby, for example, of the STRATEGIC ALLIANCE PARTNER's office or artwork for their website.

Trained Staff

If the STRATEGIC ALLIANCE PARTNER has a staff, they should be trained and educated on the benefits of coaching and how to answer the basic questions the STRATEGIC ALLIANCE PARTNER's clients may ask. Train the staff exactly how to refer people to you.

Client Workshop

The STRATEGIC ALLIANCE PARTNER invites their clients to a workshop that you provide on a regular basis.

Initial Announcement

Once you have an agreement with the STRATEGIC ALLIANCE PARTNER, we recommend that an initial communication be sent to the STRATEGIC ALLIANCE PARTNER's database. You and the STRATEGIC ALLIANCE PARTNER can craft an exciting and powerful direct mail piece that announces the alliance, introduces you, articulates the benefits of your services and offers a Complimentary Session. Be creative with this! Perhaps you offer a telelcass or free workshop. The key is to create excitement and provide opportunities for the existing clientele to experience you. It is important that the initial announcement be written or co-authored by the STRATEGIC ALLIANCE PARTNER, as he / she is the person who has credibility with his / her clients.

Ongoing Contact

It is important that the STRATEGIC ALLIANCE PARTNER's clients be reminded occasionally about your services. An excellent way to do this is to co-author a monthly newsletter. Or you could send out an email inviting the STRATEGIC ALLIANCE PARTNER's clients to subscribe for your newsletter. You can also sponsor creative things such as monthly workshops, forums, teleclasses, etc.

Formalizing Your Strategic Alliance

We strongly recommend you have the terms of your Strategic Alliance posted on your website or in a written agreement. While your written agreement can take many forms, a simple Letter of Agreement that outlines the terms of the Strategic Alliance agreement and is signed by both parties is an easy and effective way to document the specific details of your partnership.

Your Letter of Agreement should address these key areas:

- Strategic Alliance Commitment

- Your Commitments

- Compensation

- Training

- Marketing / Promotion of Alliance

Notes:

Plan Your Strategic Alliance Strategy

Hopefully you see the benefit of forming Strategic Alliances. Use the following page to plan out your next steps and then get to work!

My objectives or goals for creating a powerful, win-win-win Strategic Alliance are:

_____

_____

_____

_____

_____

Some of the reasons why I am excited about this are:

_____

_____

_____

_____

_____

_____

Some potential types of Strategic Alliance Partners are:

_____

_____

_____

_____

_____

_____

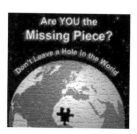

Some specific people I know who could be a Strategic Alliance Partner are:

_____

_____

_____

_____

_____

Some of the ways I could "reward" my STRATEGIC ALLIANCE PARTNER are:

_____

_____

_____

_____

_____

My next steps are:

_____

_____

_____

The concerns or challenges I have about Strategic Alliances are:

_____

_____

_____

My strategies to overcome any concerns or challenges are:

_____

_____

_____

Implementation and Evaluation

Use the chart to create a timeline for working on forming Strategic Alliances. In the TARGET DATE column indicate when you want to do each task. Use the ACTUAL DATE column to indicate when you actually complete it and then "check it off!"

Evaluation

Every 90 days, you and your partner should evaluate the partnership. Both partners should see and receive the value from the relationship.

Both parties should answer these questions:

1. The value my company has received from our strategic alliance.

2. The value I believe you have received from our strategic alliance.

3. Improvement action steps we plan to take to improve our performance in our alliance relationship.

4. Improvement action steps we would like to see you take to improve our alliance relationship.

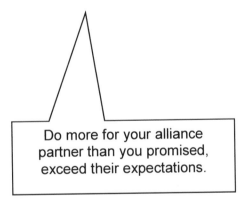

Do more for your alliance partner than you promised, exceed their expectations.

Strategic Timeline

Week 1	Identify general STRATEGIC ALLIANCE PARTNERs
	Find specific STRATEGIC ALLIANCE PARTNERs
	Identify ways to "reward" STRATEGIC ALLIANCE PARTNERs
Week 2	Write Inquiry Letter
	Send Inquiry Letter
	Make Follow-Up Phone Calls
	Schedule 1st mtgs
	Follow calls to those you did not reach - schedule 1st mtg
Week 3	Have Initial Meetings
	Send thank you note
	Follow up to answer questions
Week 4	Create a Written Agreement
	Provide service promised
	Send an Initial Announcement
Week 5	Schedule follow-up mtg with Partner in 90 days from start of partnership
	Schedule partnership evaluation every 90 days thereafter
Week 7	It is time to repeat the process and start over from the beginning.

Should repeat every two months.

Have a one-time product or service you want help promoting?

Here is a sample letter.

Dear {Mr/Mrs. business owner}:

I have a rather unusual proposition for you.

My name is {Your Name} and I'm a {your occupation} right here in {your city} since {date you opened}. During this time, I've been lucky enough to serve {#} {customers/families}.

Just recently, I was thinking of a way to market my {business/practice} in a cost-effective manner. And I realized I could do something that would be an excellent opportunity for you to gain enormous goodwill from your {clients/customers} while we both benefit.

Would you agree that in today's economy it is important to continue to bring value to our clients?

I am in the position to let you give your clients a very valuable service from me, which will greatly endear your clients to you without costing you a dime.

Let me explain.

I would like to send a letter coming from you giving your clients a coupon for a free {product/ consultation/service} with me. During this time, I'll thoroughly {explain benefits of free gift}. This service normally costs {$xxxx}.

Don't you think that would be a great thank you gift from you?

And it will not cost you a dime or take any of your time. In fact, I will pay 100% for all the postage and printing. Plus, I'll write the entire letter for you and you can have complete editorial control of it.

Please remember, this will in no way take away or be competitive with your services. I just figured it would make an excellent gift you can give away to your clients for their business and a way for me to get more people into my {business/practice}. There are no strings attached and your clients have no obligation to ever use my {product/services} again.

If this sounds like a good idea (and it really is), I'd be happy to give you a free {product/consultation/service} so you can see for yourself how great this {product/service} really is.

Just call me at {xxx-xxx-xxxx} and I'll explain everything in full detail.

Sincerely,

{Your Name}

Sample letter for partner to send

Dear {First Name},

Why would a {your occupation} write to you about a {business being endorsed}?

It's because I felt it was so important that you find out about {business being endorsed}. You know there aren't too many businesses nowadays that meet your expectations, let alone exceed them. But {name of business} has done just that.

And that's why I wanted to personally introduce you to {business owner's name}, the owner of {business}.

For {#} years now, {First Name} has {tell about what they've done for you and any exceptional work}.

And since I know every business owner is looking for ways to improve the bottom line, I asked {First Name} if {he/she} could let me do something special for you, my clients and friends. After a bit of "friendly persuasion," {he/she} agreed!

So here's the deal: When you mention this letter to {First Name}, you'll get a {complimentary or discount off} {product or service}! I've enclosed a brochure so you could see what {First Name} has to offer.

Take a look at it and then call {Business name} right away. You'll be glad you did.

Sincerely,

{Your name}

Sample of email partner can send

Dear {First Name},

When's the last time I wrote you, let alone write about somebody else?

But I wanted to brag about some of the exceptional things my {Lawyer/Accountant/Printer, etc.}, {his/her name} has done for me.

{Talk about some of the good things he/she has done for you and your practice}.

As a courtesy to me, {First Name} has agreed to spend one full hour with you free of charge and dispense {his/her} best advice.

This is not a trick, and there is no obligation to ever use {his/her} services again. This is just something I persuaded {First Name} to do because I thought you could benefit from {his/her} advice just like I have.

Just give {Name} a call at {xxx-xxx-xxxx} to schedule your free consultation, and please tell {him/her} I sent you to get your free hour.

Sincerely,

{Your name}

P.S. Just last year {Name} saved me over {$xxxx.xx} on my taxes. See what {he/she} can do for you.

11. Integrity in Relationships

"Relationships are the foundation of our human existence. Strong, loving, nurturing and meaningful relationships are crucial to life. Without this human interaction, life is meaningless and incomplete. Yet, making them work effectively remains to be a bit of a mystery to most.

What if we used integrity, the state of being whole and complete, as a blueprint for how we develop and manage our relationships? Would our relationships have more substance and fewer problems?" —Sherry Jackson

Guy Riekeman, D.C., president of Life University, has used integrity for more than 20 years as the foundation for his philosophy in establishing and maintaining positive personal and professional relationships. Riekeman has passionately dedicated himself to increasing awareness and encouraging chiropractors regarding the responsibilities and outcomes of the choices they make.

"Integrity in a relationship comes down to outcomes, not an emotional or moral issue," clarifies Riekeman. *"Do you want mediocre, ill-defined relationships that end up as problems or do you want ones with the possibility of empowerment and excellence?"*

Living in integrity:

- powerful tool in self-awareness and personal conviction
- consistency in thoughts, words and actions
- true to yourself and to others
- self-respect, clarity and inner peace
- implementation of your values
- personal ownership for a state of wholeness
- lack of integrity = mediocrity
- being in integrity = empowerment and excellence

Personal Integrity

Step One: Determine your personal values and life priorities. This step requires a great deal of introspection. Go to a quiet place. Focus on and write down the following three main categories:

1. Your needs – absolutes
2. Your wants – areas of compromise
3. Your likes – preferences

Notes:

Step Two: Set up an agreement with yourself. This can be done for both professional and personal goals. Integrity means that no matter what comes up, you will honor your agreement with yourself.

Notes:

Step Three: Identify a list of the most important people in your personal and professional life. Rank these people in their order of importance to you.

Notes:

Step Four: Make agreements with each person on your list of important life relationships.

As you begin to set up agreements with each individual, discuss your personal values and priorities and how much time you have to achieve your goals. There are three ways to set up agreements with individuals: written, spoken and unstated.

Written is the clearest way, because both parties are clear on the intention and outcome. Spoken is good. However, you might later forget the intentions and outcomes. Unstated is something that is assumed by one or both and often turns out poorly.

Notes:

Step Five: Honor the agreements that you made with yourself and others. Integrity means that no matter what comes up, you honor the agreements. "The challenge is to see how far you can expand your horizon of accountability with regard to self, family and your business," says Riekeman.

Notes:

"Seven Disciplines of Excellence"

1. Surround yourself with people who call you to something "bigger."
2. Be disciplined.
3. Create a commitment big enough to dedicate your life spirit to.
4. Establish a set of values that enliven you.
5. Design a system for creativity and having integrity.
6. Call on others to be committed and accountable.
7. Acknowledge others' contributions to your life.

Building and managing integrity in a relationship requires consistency in your thoughts, words, and actions. *"It's not about being perfect nor never making a mistake,"* says Riekeman. *"It's a way of life. So, when you are out of integrity, it's about acknowledging and taking responsibility, cleaning it up and bringing your actions and self back into integrity."*

Notes:

Bringing Your Personal Strengths to the Table with Integrity

Before you can build strong relationships or a strong team, you need to know what you bring to the table:

1. Where does your genius reside?
2. Do you feel powerful? In what areas?
3. What do others thank and praise you for?
4. Who do you admire and why?
5. Are you able to communicate your vision in a compelling way? Why? Why not?
6. What are the areas where you feel you fall short?
7. Are you willing to focus on improvement?
8. Are you willing to let go of the areas where you're not strong?
9. Are you ready and willing to seize and create opportunities for the future?
10. How do your feelings affect you life, your business and your performance?
11. How do you want to **feel**?

Notes:

Integrity in Client Attraction

Marketing integrity means different things to different people, but one thing is certain - if you violate a client's sense of integrity in any way, you will lose him.

From well-known author Michael Gerber comes this true statement: "*Without integrity, marketing is left to tricks, sophistry and lies—the same devices the old trickster used with the peas and the shells on the streets of many cities: Is it here? Is it there? Where is it?*"

How do you keep your integrity intact when you communicate to your potential clients? Here are some simple suggestions:

1. Take a hard, cold look at the product or service you are offering. Would you buy it or recommend it to someone you like? You have to believe in what you are promoting.

2. Look at your advertising / marketing claims - does the product really do everything you claim it does? Do you have measurements in place as proof and examples of ROI?

3. Are there ways your product can be misused that could result in personal injury or damage? If so, are these spelled out in the packaging or contract?

4. Look at your advertising again - are there any elements to it that could be offensive?

5. Make sure you communicate accurate delivery dates / details to your clients.

6. If you find a flaw, communicate it accurately and factually, without marketing fluff.

7. If there is a problem, don' t be afraid to apologize. This is one of the major hallmarks of business integrity.

Integrity in Team Attraction

People are drawn to values and they like to feel valued. Integrity ("Walking the talk") encourages trust, trust builds respect, respect activates commitment, commitment feeds dedication, dedication strengthens work ethic, work ethic fuels productivity...

Your organization, like you, requires a purpose as well as values to guide it.
- a clear mission statement
- key values recognized and practiced

Unfortunately, many small businesses are not clear in identifying and communicating their values, or only formally focus on their missions and their values during strategic planning.

To develop a great team be sure:
- your people are aware of your organization's mission
- your team is truly guided by its values
- to fully utilize the inspirational power of being on a mission together with shared values

Lack of commitment to values is associated with:
- increased stress levels,
- harassment suits,
- theft of time and materials,
- conflict, cliques, and gossiping,
- lowered morale and severely negative impact to performance.

When a team aligns with your vision and values, they learn how to make commitments that will elevate their performance and that of their fellow teammates. They also learn how to respectfully confront one another in an effort to demand the best from each other. A team that knows how to play as a team is a force to be reckoned with.

Exercise
List 5 powerful new ways you can "walk your talk" and communicate with clarity your vision and values to your team, associates and clients.

Notes:

Conclusion

As a writer, a business owner, a seeker, you must continue to learn personally if you want your vision to grow. You are responsible to your clients to provide the best of you that you can, as well as setting up strong relationships that empower your clients.

I have provided you with powerful strategies to define your vision, orchestrate a solid plan for action to influence your target market and communicate your brand as THE expert in your niche authentically to the world.

We challenge you to take this content, the resources and tools and explore how use them for your business / project development and growth.

Enlist a powerful team to provide on-going marketing support and "Get Known" showcases: www.getei.com

Viki Winterton

Made in the USA
San Bernardino, CA
10 November 2017